12 Wings of Successful Business Leadership:

for

Military Leaders, Marketplace Professionals, and Ministry Minded Women Who Desire to Soar and Cultivate Global Impact, Influence, and Income

by

Sharon R. Harris

Dedication

This book is dedicated to my Lord and Savior Jesus Christ for giving me the wisdom to write this book. To all of the many pastors, US Air Force commanders, senior non-commissioned officers, supervisors and the many troops who have mentored me throughout my military career. I thank you all so much!

Last, but certainly not least, I want to thank the following people:

My handsome, amazing husband Steven Harris, Sr. You are my soulmate, my covering and my best friend. I'm looking forward to seeing all of the great things we will do together in the Lord.

My wonderful parents Nathaniel and Pearly Johnson for raising me to be a respectful and Godly woman. To my only living grandfather Reverend Aiken R. Ruth, I love you so much. To the Ruth, Johnson, and Harris families, thank you so much for loving me, supporting me and standing beside me.

To my wonderful spiritual papa, Prophet Sampson Amoateng, thank you for your all prayers, love and mentorship. The Blood still speaks!

To my first Social Media Coach Dawniel Winningham, aka "The Wealthspeaker," thank you for motivating me to step out on Social Media and utilize my gifts and talents.

To Dr. Frederick Jones, my Book Coach and Publishing Strategist aka "The World's Only Worthologist," thank you so much, Sir, for teaching me to write on my knees and tell my story.

TABLE OF CONTENT

FOREWORD

It's amazing to me how people enter into the sacred place of our lives orchestrated by God. I believe that for every entrance into that sacred place is for purpose. It is what we do with the entry that makes a difference, either good or bad. The impact those persons make upon our lives can be used to elevate, diminish, or destroy us. We choose, because of how we respond to those entrances.

Sharon Johnson-Harris made an entrance into my life for a very brief moment over twenty years ago quiet, reserved, a young woman who entered, said nothing personally to me, nor I to her. From time to time through visiting her family, she'd show up for worship services, until the next military leave. Those times proved to present itself a budding, growing change. Over twenty years passed and Sharon had burst into full-bloom, exploding with energy, entering into our lives filled with God's designed purpose for her to enter into many lives encouraging seeding and nurturing in order to reap an abundant harvest.

I shout out thunderous applause into the atmosphere over Sharon's divine contribution to those who have been sitting in those dark places filled with hope, but lacking someone's entry into their lives to propel them toward their designed purpose. I believe God has prepared her for this time through the writing of this book to bring about hope to those who felt hopeless - reaching, but yet not obtaining - striving, yet not thriving. She is living proof that any who would have a zeal to succeed, will reach their goal.

I am honored to be allowed to "speak a word" on behalf of this energetic, spirit-filled, anointed motivational speaker, preacher of God's

Word in the person of Sharon Johnson-Harris. May her gift catapult her to higher places in this world affecting others' lives to the highest elevation, and in the world to come eternal life in Jesus. I pray her mantra "Go Soar Fly Girl" be fruitful beyond her wildest imagination.

"But as it is written, 'Eye hath not seen, nor ear heard, neither have entered into the heart of man, the things which God hath prepared for them who love Him.'" (1 Corinthians 2:9)

Rev. Ruthie Darien-Williams, Pastor

Church of God, Varnville (South Carolina)

Introduction

Don't Go Down With The Ships

"If the highest aim of a captain were to preserve his ship, he would keep it in the port forever."

~ Thomas Aquinas

Words cannot express how excited I am to write this book. This book was birthed from my time with the Lord in prayer. I was seeking the Lord one morning during the month of September 2016. I asked Him to give me an idea regarding a good teaching series to teach my Soar Fly Girl followers on Periscope and Facebook Live that would help to impact leaders. As I began to meditate and wait for the Lord to speak, I saw the words "leader" and "leadership." I then began to look up the meaning of both words.

As I began to research, I asked the Lord what the significance of the suffix "ship" is and why the suffix "ship" was attached to certain words. I then began to focus on the word "leadership." According to www.dictionary.com, the suffix ship is derived from the "native English suffix of nouns denoting condition, character, office, skill, etc." Therefore, any word that has the suffix "ship" describes the condition, character, office, and skill of the prefix that is attached to it. I found this revelation extremely powerful when it comes to the word leadership.

Leadership is defined as:

1. The position or function of a leader, a person who guides or directs a group: ex., "He managed to maintain his leadership of the party despite heavy opposition." Synonyms: administration, management, directorship, control, governorship, stewardship, hegemony.
2. Ability to lead: As early as sixth grade, she displayed remarkable leadership potential. Synonyms: authoritativeness, influence, command, effectiveness, sway, clout.
3. An act or instance of leading, guidance, direction: ex., "They prospered under his strong leadership."
4. Leaders of a group.

Leadership often comes with a heavy cost, along with great opportunities to influence others. True effective leadership is not for the faint or weak of heart. An important characteristic of leadership is the ability to act decisively in the place of fear. This will often require you to make choices that is often not very popular nor will it "make sense" to those who follow you.

Leadership requires vision. Oftentimes, the visionary is normally the only one who clearly understands the vision. During my research, I came across an amazing article called "Burn The Ships." This article spoke about the Spanish conquistador, Captain Hernan Cortez. "Cortez was an excellent motivator. He convinced more than 500 soldiers and 100 sailors to set sail from Spain to Mexico, commanding 11 ships, to take the world's richest treasure." Here's how Cortez got the "buy in" from the rest of his men.

He took away the option of failure. It was conquer and be heroes and enjoy the spoils of victory . . . or DIE! When Cortez and his men arrived on the shores of the Yucatan, he rallied the men for one final pep talk before leading his men into battle and utters these three words that changed the course of history, "Burn the ships."

As we would have guessed, he met resistance from his men. "Burn the ships," he repeated. He then uttered these words, "If we are going home, we are going home in their ships." With that, Cortez and his men burned their own ships except one, and by burning their own ships, the commitment level of the men was raised to a whole new level. A level much higher than any of the men, including Cortez, could have ever imagined.

The ships were sunk – he kept a single ship to send back the "royal fifth" (the king of Spain claimed 20% of all treasures). Incredibly, they succeeded in this unlikely feat. In 600 years, no one else had been able to conquer the Aztecs and plunder their riches. They were able to do it simply because there was no choice, no fallback – the ships were gone; the only alternative was death."

We all have "boats" that we need to burn. These "boats" are oftentimes excuses that we hold onto in case of failure. These backup plans cripple our ability to be successful. Success will require you to step out of your comfort zone. There needs to be a time in your life where you will give yourself and your team no excuses. I am in no way advocating abuse of your team leaders. I am advocating that you get out of your own way. Many times when God directs you to do something, it will always be BIGGER than yourself and your abilities.

I cannot remember one time in life where God instructed me to do something, and it was totally "sweat less." Captain Cortez gave himself and his men no options. He was willing to risk his own life and the life of his men if required. Many disagree with Captain Cortez's leadership style, but one thing is for certain; he did succeed beyond his wildest dreams.

Visionaries are able to see where others cannot. There must come a time that you do not allow your extra boats to become an excuse not to step out and do something new. There must be a time where you burn your extra boats and not go down with them once you burn them. We all have that backup plan in case of failure but what about the having a plan if you succeed? It is always wise to plan but it is important not to make plans to fail. Many times our "ships" are fear based and not based on faith.

One of my favorite Bible scriptures is Hebrews 11: 1: Now faith is the substance of things hoped for, the evidence of things not seen. Your faith should reflect only God's ability and not just your ability, is the substance of the things "you" hoped for and the evidence of things "you" have not seen. So yes, your vision should be massive, and it should actually terrify you.

People around you are supposed to think you are crazy because your vision is GOD SIZED and NOT man size. Your vision should NEVER be about what you or what you are going to accomplish, but it should be about what God can do through you. It is important that leaders are people of faith and not of doubt and unbelief. Your trust should not rely on yourself but in God my sisters. He is bigger than any opposition you will face.

All leaders will face giants. All leaders will be faced with giant-sized opposition but your faith is the substance of what you hope for in the midst of all else. As a leader, my faith in God has lead me through much opposition in my life.

I served 21 wonderful years in the Air Force, and I would not have traded it for anything in the world. The Air Force taught me how to carry myself as a leader and how to have my own voice. As a young child, I was not very confident, and I did not see myself as a leader. The military was the furthest thing from my mind. But during my time in the military, God blessed me with some of the best mentors who really coached me. I have been blessed to win many awards and received many accolades. Now, I am very bold and confident.

During my time in the military I made many mistakes. I look at them as lessons learned and areas of further development. I did not do things perfectly, as all leaders do. Leaders, you must win the battle with yourself first, or else you will burn and go down with the very ships you must let go of.

All of us cling to something that acts as our escape hatch or our exit strategy (in the negative connotation). It's our safety net, "just in case . . ." If we were truly honest, we would say, "This is my safety net, just in case I get scared." There is nothing wrong at all with that rationale. We postpone action until we no longer feel fear. Either that, or our actions are shallow attempts never designed to succeed. In reality, we must learn to act decisively in spite of our fear."

I personally had to let go of a huge ship in my life, which was my military career. Although it was amazing and I totally loved it, I knew that God had more plans for my life. It was not easy for me to walk away from it, but I found that I was losing my passion for it. That's when I knew that God was calling me to walk away from it. It has not been an easy transition for me. The military pays very well and it has opened many doors and opportunities in my life. But the mission and the call that God has on my life is greater.

I always wanted to impact others and mentor. I especially have a passion for youth. I love talking to them about their futures and encouraging them. I especially love talking to them about military life and how it has made me a better woman and leader. My goal for this book is to draw from the many experiences that God has taken me through and cover the most important areas that leaders need to become impactful leaders. In the Air Force there are "wings" each wing included squadron and units in which personnel who performed particular functions would be placed under a particular wing. Each Air Force Base has wings. Each wing have certain personnel who perform certain functions in order to keep our air power intact. As you read this book you will discover that each chapter has a wing. These wings are the most important components of a successful and most of all influential leaders. Leaders without influence your leadership is powerless. Unless you continue to develop in your character your position will wear you down. Relationships are your most important asset as a leader. Great relationships will increase your revenue, bring divine connections and open great doors for you.

I have often said many times on social media that leadership is not about position, it is about influence. This book is going to challenge you leaders and require you to do some serious inventory regarding your life and character. I truly believe that people watch your character more than anything else. Your character and how you relate with others will carry you where money cannot take you. I truly believe this book will not just help leaders. It will transform lives.

I challenge you to look at your own life. What are the extra ships that you have carried in your life that is weighing you down and preventing you from stepping out and being that great visionary that God has called you to be? What are the extra ships that you must burn in your life that are crippling you from going into what God has for your life? How is your self talk? What do you say to yourself about yourself?

Wing # 1

Relationships

The best way to lead people in the future is to connect with them in the present.

~ James Kouzes and Barry Posner

Leadership is lifting a person's vision to high sights, raising a person's performance to a higher standard. In order to really impact those you lead, you must develop relationships with them. Trust is built upon relationships. It's very difficult to truly follow a leader that you do not trust. Success does not come from talent and wisdom alone. These are great but true success enables you to develop strong relationships with others. Truly successful people are people of relationships.

Leadership must be coupled with love. You must truly love those whom you lead. When your people know that you truly care for them, they will follow your lead. Leadership must come from a pure heart and pure motives. Leaders are often hindered, because they only want to lead certain types of people. I believe that the muscle of a leader is tested when confronted with different types of personalities.

Leaders, we must be willing to form relationships with those you follow. I am not saying that you should go to lunch with them every day or invite them to dinner every day. It's about having a concern for your people and what is going on in their daily lives and how you can assist them.

When I was in the Air Force, I was not a morning person. I hated getting up early. In my heart, I wanted to crawl back into bed as soon as I arrived at my office. I have held my share of high positions that often challenged my character. I was not perfect, but one thing I did know, was that I loved those whom I led. Even those who did not like me or understood me, I still had a love or concern for them.

I was often given the nickname of "Sunshine," because I loved to smile a lot and talk with others. There were many days my heart was broken and sad. There were jobs that I did not enjoy, which practically made me miserable, but I tried with the strength that God gave me not to allow it to totally take me over. I cannot tell you how many times I would greet my troops and co-workers and they would ask me, "Master Sergeant, you are always smiling, how do you do it?" Honestly, when I walked around greeting and chatting with my fellow airmen, it helped me so much. It helped me to escape what was going on inside of me. It helped me to focus on someone other than myself. It helped me connect with others. It made them feel that someone cared about them, even those who did not understand or agree with my methods and decisions.

According to Proverbs 3: 1-6 New Living Translation (NLT):

1 My child, never forget the things I have taught you. Store my commands in your heart.

2 If you do this, you will live many years, and your life will be satisfying.

3 Never let loyalty and kindness leave you! Tie them around your neck as a reminder. Write them deep within your heart.

4 Then you will find favor with both God and people, and you will earn a good reputation.

5 Trust in the LORD with all your heart; do not depend on your own understanding.

6 Seek his will in all you do, and he will show you which path to take.

I so love this passage. This is a powerful verse to meditate on and post in your office, sun visor, or mirror as a reminder. This scripture gives you a powerful key to have favor with God and man. You must tie loyalty and kindness around your neck. It needs to be a foundation in your character and leadership style. This is what cause people to want to connect with you and follow your lead. There is a time that we must be firm in leadership but there is also a time that we should display loyalty and kindness to those we lead.

You strengthen these characteristics by spending time in the presence of the Lord. Leaders must have an ear to hear the direction of the Lord. The Lord know what lies ahead of you. You must always place Him on top of your agenda. You must never depend on your own understanding. You must acknowledge Him in all that you do.

Pride is one of the greatest enemy to leaders. Some of us cannot handle positions of authority. Leadership comes with a great burden. It comes with a great price. You MUST have the presence and the anointing of the Lord.

Leaders must be people of relationships. The first relationship that you MUST have is with the Lord and the second type of relationships that you must have is with others which includes your family, those you lead, and your friends. Your relationship with the Lord will determine your relationship with others. Leaders, this is a facet of leadership that many leaders are not aware of. But today, you are highly favored by God because now you will receive more knowledge, so that you will grow in favor with God and man. This is one of the most important chapters in this book.

Effective leadership will require that you make an effort to get to know those who are around you whom you lead. Proverbs 27:23-24 NLT says:

23 Know the state of your flocks, and put your heart into caring for your herds,

24 for riches don't last forever, and the crown might not be passed to the next generation.

You must show concern for your flock. You have a legacy to pass on. You cannot pass it on without knowing the condition of your "flock." This scripture is not just for pastors. It's for everyone. This scripture pertains to your finances, your family and any other thing or person assigned to be under your influence or guardianship.

I worked for many amazing commanders, and I really learned this first hand from a female Squadron Commander that I worked for. She had an uncanny knack for always knowing what was going on with her people. Her memory was amazing!! For six months I had the pleasure to work with a Lieutenant Colonel, and I was always amazed by her. I performed as her Squadron Superintendent and her right hand. I assisted her with managing over 180 members. I cannot tell you how many times she would always talk about her Airmen and how she cared about them. Due to her ranking position, she could not show too much unprofessionalism, but one thing I saw that I loved about her was that she loved her people. When they hurt, she hurt. She was very firm and did everything by the book, but she always thought carefully before she did things.

During my time with her, I learned the importance of connecting with those whom you lead. I loved the fact that she kept up with everybody's birthday. She hated when someone had a birthday, and she did not know. She loved to celebrate others on their special day. She often told me that she was not a "people" person or that she was shy. But to me, she was bold and very compassionate.

On her Airmen's birthdays, she personally wrote birthday cards to everyone on their special day. I loved that about her! Once a week, she and I would do our weekly walk-arounds to talk to our fellow Airmen. She made sure to block off her calendar so that she could greet her Airmen. I personally watched her go to each Airman from the highest ranking to the lowest ranking and ask them how they were doing or what plans they had for the upcoming weekend.

I loved her memory!! She remembered a lot of details about her people. If an Airman had anything going on personally with a family member, she would always asked about how they are doing. She was brilliant. She taught me to be concerned about your people. She taught me to be attentive and to listen to others. Ma'am I know you are reading this book, and I thank you so much for everything you have taught me! I salute you!! You have mentored me and taught me so much! I'm forever grateful!

Honestly, it took me a long time to catch on to this. I used to think that because I am a leader that I did not have to connect with my people. Now I know that is the worst thing I could do as a leader. God allowed me to become a Squadron Superintendent to serve under that commander so that I can learn to connect with others which is one of the most important aspects of leadership.

I hope that from what you have read so far that you understand the importance of connecting with those whom you lead. Here are some tips to help you connect with those you are leading:

1. Walk in integrity. A great leader is a leader who operates in integrity. She does not show respect of persons. They do not say one thing and do another. Do what's right and be honest,

no matter who is looking. Rest assured your team is watching and listening.

2. Make sure that you do not display any perception of favoritism. Favoritism breeds division. Be honest but fair. Honesty is telling the truth to others. Integrity is telling the truth to yourself.

3. Make every interaction with those you lead count: Those members that you lead are not just your laborers, they are your co-laborers. Be sure to form positive relationships with your team. Remember, they are there to help you achieve the vision. Spend time connecting with your people and getting to know them. Leaders must be selfless. Be sure to greet your people and display genuine interest in your people.

4. Be cognizant of your facial expressions and mannerisms when interacting with your people. If you are in a bad mood, be sure to get your emotions together so that you do not take it out on your people.

5. Take care of the needs of your team. Are you the kind of leader in which your team members can come to you and have confidence that you would assist them? Leaders are listeners. Be sure to refer your team members to the proper agencies so that they can receive the proper help. If you have the ability to help them, by all means help them. Five years ago I served under a great squadron commander at Los Angeles Air Force Base, California who said "when you take care of your people, they will take care of the mission." Bless your people and recognize them publicly when they do well.

6. Keep your hands clean. Leaders should never gossip with their team members about other team members or upper leadership. Leaders should never be the center of any gossip. Do not gossip about your people. It is funny that oftentimes when

those under a leader can gossip, it doesn't go very far, but when a leader gossips, it spreads like a wildfire.

7. Never discuss your deep personal problems with your team members. Leaders, if you need counseling regarding personal issues, make sure you seek it from someone trustworthy outside of your team. Do not just set the standard but be the standard! Notice that in scripture Jesus often spent time away by Himself to pray and seek the face of the Father. Jesus was not dependent on others. He was only dependent on His Father.

8. Embrace feedback. Leaders are very good about giving feedback but terrible at receiving feedback. Feedback will only make you a more well-rounded leader. Again, become a leader who listens to your people. Tell your people, "Thank you." This will really help you when there are disagreements between yourself and your team. Everyone is not "wrong".

9. Many leaders have wounded their followers and are unaware. A wise leader is aware that they have faults and does something about it. This includes apologizing (smile) and asking for forgiveness. Many times leaders, people are unhappy because of mistreatment (whether it is true or perceived). Leaders, it is your responsibility to get rid of any discord. Leaders, you must learn to communicate clearly with your people. You must learn to form your words in such a way that you correct any wrong behavior and not destroy a person's character.

10. Allow your co-laborers to use their talents. God is so wise and all knowing that HE does not allow one man or woman to have all of the answers. God made all of us with different talents and ability. The wrong person with the wrong ability will destroy a business, company or ministry. You must know your people so that you can ensure that they are placed in the right place at the right time. When people are placed in the right area and can utilize their talent it will bring a sense of fulfilment and

cohesion to the team. Once again, you have to make sure that person has the character and personality to operate in the area you need them to fill.

Proverbs 29:14 NLT says, *If a king judges the poor fairly, his throne will last forever.* This scripture drives home the fact that as a leader, you must treat your people fairly. You must have clean hands! We see in scripture that any king who judges the poor fairly will last on his throne forever. In other words, he will not be overthrown. He will have influence on his people forever.

Leaders, you must lead everyone fairly. Not only just to the rich but also to the poor. You must not be a respecter of persons. You must not have favorites. You must be careful of the perception of favoritism. You must not allow one person to get away with wrong and punish another. You must rule and govern from a place of fairness, compassion, excellence and love.

Leaders, you must not compromise. You must always posture yourself in God to obey, no matter the cost.

Leaders, we must be careful not to burn bridges. What I loved about the Air Force is that it is a huge network. I learned to form relationships with others. I always tried to connect with people who performed jobs that I did not do so that if I needed anything, I could ask them questions. I did the same thing for others. As I connected with people who performed different jobs, I was sure to let them know that if I could do anything for them, to let me know; in turn, they did the same for me. I did not form networks to use people. I made sure that they could benefit from my expertise as well. Leaders, it's time to become bridge builders and not bridge burners.

Wing #2

Mentorship

A mentor is someone who sees more talent and ability within you than you see in yourself.

~ Bob Proctor

Mentorship is a relationship in which a more experienced or more knowledgeable person helps to guide a less experienced or less knowledgeable person. A truly good and effective mentor is very hard to find. Every good leader needs to have someone to show them the ropes. It is important to choose the right kind of mentor.

Selecting a mentor should be done with a lot of prayer and discernment. Everyone is not equipped to speak into your life. The right mentor can help you to go your next level. I'm so thankful that during my time in the Air Force, I came across so many mentors.

The Air Force taught me that, as a leader, you are to mentor and help develop those Airmen who are under your leadership. The Air Force taught me that you must first be an expert at your craft and then you supervise others.

The one thing that was not taught through Air Force regulations was how to develop my character to mentor. I had to learn this first hand by trial and error. I began to watch those officers and enlisted airmen who were great mentors. I have encountered some of the best of the best. The first person who impacted me was a female African-American Master Sergeant (E-7) whom I met during the 1990s. I was an E-1 (Airman Basic) fresh into the Air Force with no stripes on my arms, but when I met this sharp female Senior Non-Commissioned Officer with the many stripes on her arms, I was impacted. I watched how she always kept her uniform sharp and always carried herself with confidence, yet with humility.

I remember when I met her, I immediately liked her. She was very kind and very knowledgeable in her job. She also had an amazing work ethic. She treated me wonderfully. She was always encouraging me and building me up. She spoke to and saw the future leader inside of me. She did not talk to me like I was beneath her. This is when I knew I met my first military mentor.

Your mentor should be a person who has been where you want to go. Your mentor should be a person of humility, integrity and greatness. Your mentor should always see the greatness that God has placed in you and help you to bring it forth. Many mentors struggle with jealousy towards their mentees. If you are a mentor, you should never envy or hold back those you are mentoring. Mentees, if your mentor tries to smother you and operates towards you in hostility, they are not your mentors.

Many of us lead by how we were taught. We lead by what we have seen in others. All of us have been impacted by someone whether positively or negatively. God is so amazing. God has set up the home to be the primary place of mentorship. Parents have a great responsibility to mentor and develop their children. Parents, it is your responsibility to see the God-given ability, talents and gifts inside your children, cultivate and correct their character, and point them in the direction where God has for them to go.

The Bible says in Proverbs 22:6, "Start children off on the way they should go, and even when they are old they will not turn from it." Parents, you are your child's first mentor. You are the one who must help your children develop their God-given potential. Parents must seek God first about the direction of their child's life and then point and train the child in that direction. Parents, we must not force our will on our children but God's will.

When parents are not in a child's life, they end up going in a different direction. Parents, you must speak life into your children. With the help of God, they will and can be redirected into His purpose for their lives. God does this many times by sending someone into their lives to help them get back on the right path.

Leaders, you need mentorship in your life. Many leaders want to be lone rangers. If you are a leader who refuses mentorship, you are crippling your growth. When it comes to mentorship, you must not enter into it lightly. When you are mentored by someone you are receiving an impartation from the person who is mentoring you. You must be sure to watch the fruit of the person from whom you are receiving mentorship.

On the other hand, leaders, you must first humble yourself to receive instruction from the mentor that God has placed in your life. Many mentees fight their mentors. If you are under a mentor and you are feeling friction or uncomfortable, seek God and ask him for his direction. You must always go upward for counsel. You must always seek someone with wisdom for advice and not always your friends and peers.

Here are 12 keys to finding the right mentor, please take your time and study these points:

1. A God assigned mentor will see the potential in you and pull it out. It's their job to help sharpen you and not abuse you. Any mentor who verbally abuses you and crushes your spirit and causes you to think less of yourself is not a good mentor. The right mentor will correct you and not leave you wounded. They will not only cut you when needed but also sew up and help you to heal as well.

2. They will not compete with you nor hold you back. The right mentor will not try to take your spotlight. They will truly love you and see your gifts and talents and allow you to be yourself. They will not hold you back nor change who you are to please them. They will help you prepare for the spotlight. They will use their influence to help you and not control you. The worst kind of mentor is a controlling one.

3. A good mentor will not control your will and everyday life. They will allow you to have your own identity and help you with the areas you are weak in. They will respect your free will. Never lose your identity to serve a mentor. If a mentor feels you are not ready for something, they will help you to prepare for it. God is not a controller and neither should your mentor become one.

4. A good mentor will not allow you to worship them. They will point you to God and show you the greatness that God has placed in you. We should never worship another man or woman. We respect them and honor them but never make them into a god. Keep in mind that just as God has blessed your mentor, He can and will bless you too! My spiritual papa Prophet Sampson Amoateng always says, *"You do not need the man, but you need the God of the man."* On the other hand, I also met many mentors who impacted me and did not serve God.

5. Please hear me when I say this: *There is nothing wrong with learning from those who do not believe as you do.* I am not saying to go against

your morals. I am saying to chew the meat and spit out the bones. You must be well rounded. You must be able to sit in the midst of great people whether they are in Church or out of Church. God can use you to impact them. Never ever compromise your relationship with the Lord. Many people are placed in your life to be informants but not necessarily mentors.

6. Watch the life of your mentor. Are they truthful? Are they integral? Are they faithful in their marriage and relationships? Are they givers? Are they compassionate? You must be able to see past your possible mentor's success and see their character. In order to do this, you must be quiet and observe their life. Become a fruit inspector, not to judge but to make sure you are under the right person. You want to make sure you have fruit as well. Do not operate as a dirty or shady mentee. Sometimes your mentor may have ways that you do not agree with. Still, in that you can learn. I have learned a lot from my mentors' mistakes. There are no perfect mentors. None.

7. There should be a mutual love between both of you. There should be a love and respect between you and your mentor. There should be an instant connection when you are with your mentor. Seeing and being in the presence of your mentor should bring a smile to your face. It should be a sense of excitement when you are in the presence of your mentor. Whenever you leave your mentor, you should be ready to move on to the next level. The right mentor will strengthen you, pray for you, and cover you.

8. When you are in the presence of your mentor, it should not be to gossip or waste their time. It should be to receive instruction and impartation. Successful mentors do not have time to waste. Respect your mentor and do not waste their time. Come into their midst with a pen and a piece of paper ready to learn, listen, and take notes. If you have questions, write them down. Be a

person of excellence. Be prepared. Truly successful people do not waste time. They guard their time. Do not be a difficult or rebellious mentee. Be ready and focused.

9. Make time to meet with your mentor at least once a week or month. This should be the time to receive knowledge and to brainstorm ideas for your next move. When you are given things to do by your mentor to go to the next level, do it!! Leave your ego at the door!! If they do not share or pour into you, then they are not your mentor. A mentor should seek to give and not just take.

10. Any mentor who does not want to share with you or make themselves available to you, they are NOT your mentor. The right mentor will make time to sharpen you. The right mentor will cause you to feel charged and revived when you leave their presence. Proverbs 27:17 says, *As iron sharpens iron, so one person sharpens another.*

11. Your mentor must be at a level where you want to go!!! Your mentor must be a person of experience. I always seek out people who are operating on levels that are higher than myself. You must be with people of influence. It will pull your mentality up! You must love who God has created you to be and place yourself around greatness. Are you a pastor? Seek a pastor who is more successful/seasoned than you are and operating on a higher a level. Are you a business woman or aspiring to be one? Seek those who have the same type of business and are successful at it.

12. Do not copy or steal ideas from your mentor. Listen to the voice of God and let Him download ideas into you. Ask God to give you your own ideas. Your mentor can also give you ideas to help you, as well, but don't copy ideas from your mentor without speaking with them first.

Some of you have not met your God-assigned mentor as of yet. Do not be discouraged, but rejoice! You now have enough knowledge to recognize the right mentor! Below are some tips you can use until your mentor arrives:

1. Watch and pray. Ask the Lord to bring the right mentor into your life. Along with praying, you must keep your eyes and ears open to recognize the right one.
2. Invest in yourself. This includes reading books, listening to audiobooks, and viewing podcasts. Fill yourself with information regarding the direction to which you aspire.
3. Take business, leadership or self-improvement courses. Seek out courses that will arm you with knowledge.
4. Attend conferences and seminars. Seek out leadership, business, or ministry seminars and events. These events alone can open doors for you to meet successful people in the area you are looking for expertise. You must place yourself in the atmosphere to meet the one assigned for you.

Mentorship is a ship that leaders cannot afford to miss. Mentors will help you to get out of your own head. You need iron that will sharpen you. You are on your way to greatness, and God has great people assigned to impact your life.

I will never forget when Evangelist Dr. Mike Murdock said during a teaching that, "When God wants to do things in your life, He often uses a person." Meeting the right mentor will change your life. If you are (currently) mentoring someone, you now have the keys to become an even better one.

Wing #3

Craftsmanship

Do you see someone skilled in their work? They will serve before kings; they will not serve before officials of low rank. Proverbs 22:29 (NIV)

A craftsman is defined as a person who practices or is highly skilled in a craft; artist. According to Huffington Post, "Successful leaders should treat their leadership as a craft to be carefully honed and ever improving. The better we become, the more our competence and depth of character combine to form the most helpful contributions moment to moment."

Self-improvement is pivotal to transforming into a better leader. Leadership is a craft. It takes the power of God and skill in order to lead and perform effectively. Anyone can give directions but only a few truly lead. Leadership requires craftsmanship. There is an art to leading and influencing people. Without influence, you are ineffective as a leader. This is why you must always seek to improve and become better. Every leader, no matter how long they have been a leader, will need to have a tune up every now and then. No matter what area you may be leading in, you must master it. You must be knowledgeable. Leaders, you must always seek to become more knowledgeable.

In the Air Force there are skill levels in every Air Force Specialty Codes or (jobs) that every Airman performs. Three skill levels are labeled as Apprentices; five skill levels are labeled as Journeymen; and seven skill levels are called Craftsmen. Every person has a "training record." This record has a list of all required areas that must be mastered within your job to become a Journeyman or Craftsman. Every job may have hundreds of tasks that every person must master in order to go to the next level of expertise in a particular job.

Each promotion requires a certain skill level, which is gained through Career Development Courses that use training guides for specific jobs. These books are just like training manuals.

Some of these tasks require only familiarization of Air Force Regulations and/or actual hands-on performance of that particular task. In order for you to be "fully qualified" to perform a task, your trainer must see you perform that task proficiently. You are required to initial off on that task, and then they would also initial next to the trainee's initials certifying that you are indeed proficient in those tasks. Every Airman's goal is to progress from Apprentice to Craftsman skill levels. Craftsmen have mastered all the required tasks and now have enough experience to train others that are coming up behind them. They are "deemed" as the experts in their craft.

The amazing thing about this is that every Journeyman and Craftsman must first have their training records scrutinized by the Airman's supervisor, flight commander (as needed), training manager and squadron commander. The person who has the most important role in upgrade training is the supervisor. The supervisors mentors the young Airmen through every task to ensure they have mastered those tasks before certifying they are fully qualified. The most important thing is that the supervisor must first be fully qualified and proficient. It is an insult to lead or supervise others and not be qualified or knowledgeable. You cannot have a high ranking or position and have a low skill level or knowledge. High ranking with a low skill level signifies incompetence!

The best leaders are those who have expertise. I totally understand that you cannot be a know it all. When it comes to your craft, you must master it. When it comes to your ministry, business, household or whatever you put your hands to, you need to become knowledgeable. Leaders, surround yourself with people with knowledge. Once God brings those people into your life to help you with the vision, learn from them. You are not to take over their job but learn from them and expand your knowledge.

When a vision is from God, He will add people to help you and provide the right skills you need to finish what He has for you to do. You must not be the type of leader who is totally hands off. If you do not learn how things are supposed to be done efficiently, you will not be able to recognize the cracks. Moses (leaders), you must go up into the mountain to commune with God, but there must also come a time that you must come down and lead your people. Leaders, we cannot stay in the clouds all day, every day or on our thrones in our offices and not engage with your people.

On the other hand, leaders you need the kind of people in place so that when you are on the mountain or away on vacation, the vision will still move forward and will not become stagnant or derail from its original course. Incompetence must cease leaders! You must trust your people and not micromanage. But you must always be in a posture to learn. You cannot depend on you and your ideas alone. God wants to bring people of excellence into your life. Do not fight excellence, embrace it.

In order to be great, there must be constant improvement. Your church, business or organization should be better because you are there. When you, as a leader, do not take time to investigate what is going on with yourself, your people and your ministry, everything will suffer. Your ministry, business or organization cannot be any greater than your connection to God. This includes your leadership, connections, and the people who are working along with you (co-laborers). Many churches, businesses, careers and homes are destroyed because of a lack of knowledge. Once knowledge arrives, ignorance must go! Ignorance is crippling your organization, ministry, career, and business. Come off ignorance and embrace your God given craft. Your organization should constantly be thriving, multiplying and growing.

No church, ministry, business or organization can be greater than the head. Your leadership position is not just for you! It's not for you to flounce or walk in pride; it is for you to impact others for Him! As you take care of your people and the things that concern God, He will take care of you. Every person you are leading/managing is an assignment from God. Your leadership craft is increased when you place the right people in the right places. This is why you must know your people so you will recognize their gift and place them in the right position so that their God given ability will come alive. The right person in the right position will bless your business and ministry beyond your wildest dreams.

The Lord showed me a powerful scripture that really shows the power of craftsmanship and having the right person in the right position. In Exodus 31 we get a glimpse of directions that God gave to Abraham while he was on the mountain with Him for 40 days and 40 nights. God gives Moses specific instructions regarding the tabernacle.

Here is the text from Exodus 31: 1-11:

1 Then the LORD said to Moses, 2 "See, I have chosen Bezalel son of Uri, the son of Hur, of the tribe of Judah, 3 and I have filled him with the Spirit of God, with wisdom, with understanding, with knowledge and with all kinds of skills — 4 to make artistic designs for work in gold, silver and bronze, 5 to cut and set stones, to work in wood, and to engage in all kinds of crafts. 6 Moreover, I have appointed Oholiab, son of Ahisamak, of the tribe of Dan, to help him. Also I have given ability to all the skilled workers to make everything I have commanded you: 7 the tent of meeting, the ark of the covenant law with the atonement cover on it, and all the other furnishings of the tent — 8 the table and its articles, the pure gold lampstand and all its accessories, the altar of incense, 9 the altar of burnt offering and all its utensils, the basin with its stand — 10 and also the woven garments, both the sacred garments for Aaron the priest and the garments for his sons when they serve as priests, 11 and the anointing oil and fragrant incense for the Holy Place. They are to make them just as I commanded you."

In this scripture, you will see that Bezalel was a skilled artist who was filled with the Spirit of God who had the ability to do specific work for the tabernacle and the Ark of the Covenant. God always gives specific instructions on how He wants things to be done. God also anointed Oholiab and skilled workers to help with building items required for the tabernacle. This alone was an amazing honor to build for the tabernacle. This was very place where the priest would come to offer animal sacrifices to worship God. The Holy Place was where the presence of the Lord dwelled. God always makes provision for the vision. God already had the right people in the midst of Moses to bring His vision to past. It was God who opened the eyes of Moses as to whom was around him.

Leaders, ask the Lord to open your eyes so that you can see the gifts in those who are around you. If you remember, at the beginning of this chapter, one of the definitions of craftsman is an artist. There are craftsmen in your midst, and God wants to increase your own personal craftsmanship. God wants to design something beautiful in your life, business and ministry.

Some of you leaders have the wrong people in the wrong positions. Some of you may have placed them there because of pity or as a favor and not by the leading of the Lord. I encourage you to look at your staff, ministry, or business. Make the necessary changes. Are your people operating in places where they are gifted? Could it be that they may not be performing the way they should be because they are not operating in an area that fits them? Is it possible leaders that with further training they could flourish even the more? Leaders, you must help your people cultivate, grow and use their gifts. The wrong person placed in wrong place will unleash disaster in your ministry, business or organization. Know your people and master your craft, ladies. If you are in ministry, study ministry; if you are in business, study business. Master your craft, craftsman!

Wing #4

Followership

Followership does not mean changing the rank of followers but changing their response to their rank, their response to their superiors and to the situation at hand.

~ Barbara Kellerman

It is the men behind who make the man ahead.

~ Merle Crowell

Followership is defined as: 1) Following; and 2) The capacity or willingness to follow a leader. Followership is an important ship that many leaders overlook. Followership is the ability to get behind a program or a vision, to be part of a team, and then bring results that are expected. It is important for any successful leader or a follower to be able to take directions well.

Followership often receives a bad rap! How well the followers follow is as important as how well a leader leads. Any organization, ministry or business which lacks followership will not have many results. Leaders must not only lead, they must follow. They must humble themselves and follow as well as lead.

Followership does not mean you are less than anyone. Followership signifies that you are a person of humility. Everyone must follow someone. We follow the laws of government, so why not follow those who were placed over you? In Scripture, we see the story of Elijah and Elisha. We see the significance of Elijah throwing his cloak over Elisha. Let read the now read the scripture?

1 Kings 19:19-21

19 So Elijah went from there and found Elisha, son of Shaphat. He was plowing with twelve yoke of oxen, and he himself was driving the twelfth pair. Elijah went up to him and threw his cloak around him. 20 Elisha then left his oxen and ran after Elijah. "Let me kiss my father and mother goodbye," he said, "and then I will come with you." "Go back," Elijah replied. "What have I done to you?" 21 So Elisha left him and went back. He took his yoke of oxen and slaughtered them. He burned the plowing equipment to cook the meat and gave it to the people, and they ate. Then he set out to follow Elijah and became his servant.

As we read this passage of scripture, we see the Prophet Elijah throwing his mantle on Elisha. This action symbolized a mentor casting his mantle on a mentee. The Lord desires to pour Himself out upon us. He desires that we "take His yoke and learn of Him." Elijah was led by the spirit of God to cast his cloak of spiritual authority onto his next protege. As we previously read in the passage, Elisha responded initially to Elijah that he wanted to go back and kiss his family. Elijah responded, "Go back, what have I to do with you?" Elijah was letting Elisha know that he was not the one who called him, God was the one.

Elisha was receiving a golden opportunity to follow Elijah or stay with the oxen. To me, the oxen represents labor; the oxen also represents what he has been doing many years. It was a source of income and how he made a living. Elisha had to choose whether or not he was going to let go of what he was comfortable with or was he willing to launch out by faith and become a servant and follow Elijah. Elisha was presented with an opportunity to be trained under one of the greatest prophets of all time.

Although Elijah performed many miracles through the power of God, he came to a place where he was getting weary in the faith. The Lord was looking for a man with a servant's heart to continue where Elijah would leave off. I love how Elisha responded. He slaughtered his oxen and burned the plowing equipment and gave it to the people. Elisha chose to burn and give away all that he had to follow his mentor.

Leaders, in your business or ministry always look to transfer the mantle onto someone else who is trainable and has a servant's heart. In the Air Force, anytime I had to learn a new position or lead a new section due to the previous leader's upcoming change of assignment, I had to perform what was called "shadowing." During the shadowing process, I had to either spend half days or whole work hours one to five days a week with the person that I was replacing. The person I was replacing had to teach me all of their daily duties and provide me with instruction manuals so that I could learn the rules and regulations for my new position so that I could work my way up to performing it independently. Shadowing can last anywhere from one to six weeks. Shadowing is so much more helpful because it allows you to practice walking in your new position.

Leaders, you must decide to follow. The Lord will not make you do anything. Many of you desire to go higher, but many leaders struggle with following. Following is the bridge to leading. By becoming a follower, I was able to glean under some great military leaders. It was through following that I was able to connect with my Lord and Savior. You cannot receive if you do not follow. You cannot grow unless you are following the right person and listening to the right voice. Leaders, you must follow the one who has the voice for your life.

Wing #5

Stewardship

Moreover, it is required in stewards that a man be found faithful.

~1 Corinthians 4:2 King James Version (KJV)

L eaders must be responsible. They must own their areas of responsibility whether it's family, business, or ministry. They must tend to it, feed it, and nurture it so that it can grow into full maturity. Stewardship is defined as: 1) the office, duties, and obligations of a steward; and 2) the conducting, supervising, or managing of something; especially the careful and responsible management of something entrusted to one's care.

This even entails taking care of not only yourself but also your people. We must go beyond just doing our jobs. We must take care of our people. You must be sure that you do not lose your influence. Being a leader is similar to being a shepherd. Shepherds have all kinds of sheep and although they may often run or wander away from the fold, it is the shepherd's responsibility to take care of them and protect them from danger. As a leader, I know firsthand how difficult it can be leading others. I understand the frustration of trying to lead/manage people with different personalities and opinions. Heck, I even understand how frustrating it can be when trying to lead yourself, along with trying to lead others. But trust me when I tell you that if you are reading this book, you have what it takes to get the job done. As a matter of fact, God has already given you all that you need to handle whatever comes your way.

Leadership is an ever growing inward art and everyday is a new day to learn and discover something new. It will take constant observation and the willingness to readjust and remove and tweak methods that does not work. I personally believe that leaders who master themselves and their behavior are 99% on their way to next level. The remaining percent is dealing with people.

A leader who has herself under control wins major victories. I am not overlooking the challenges of leading others. But again, it is all about setting boundaries, standards and maintaining them. If your business or ministry is not flowing properly, that means there are some deficiencies with your organization. Those whom you lead must know what your expectations or rules of engagement are. The expectations must be clearly set. Most importantly, I highly recommend that you put your expectations and rules of engagement on paper. Those who follow you must know what is required of them. This alone will protect you if you have the difficult job of releasing them.

We must not expect people to follow standards and procedures if we have not made them clear. Your vision cannot grow unless there is some planting, watering, pruning and uprooting, if necessary. Remember this is your ministry, business or organization. Therefore, you must constantly be aware of what's going on within your organization.

Do not be an absentee leader. Do not be the type of leader where people must hunt you down to get the help that they need. Remember, this is your vision. So begin to take steps to be more invested in it.

During my assignment at Minot Air Force Base, all clinic leaders had to attend a mandatory meeting on Monday mornings at 8:00 a.m., which was called AM Openers. Actually, I loved the concept of it. During this meeting, the head leadership of the clinic sat at the head table and the remaining section leadership, such as Section Commanders and Flight

Chiefs, sat in available seating. Seated at the head table was our head Commander who was a full bird female Colonel. She was amazing. She was very intelligent and a focused and intent listener.

During our weekly meetings, all section leaders would get up, one by one, to brief the Colonel on events that happened during the past week. They would bring their victories as well as their challenges. The Colonel gave every member in the room an opportunity to speak. She often called these opportunities, "around the room." These meetings were very informative and important to the Colonel because it allowed her to hear what is going on with the people within the clinic.

Sometimes, during these meetings, things are brought to her attention where changes needed to be made in certain policies. One of the many things I liked about her was that she defended her people and would not allow others outside of the clinic to bad mouth us. This is how any leader should be when it comes to their organization. They should never allow people outside of their organization to talk negatively about it.

People are entitled to their opinions but never join in with them and talk bad about what's been placed in your hands. Even if the person who stated their opinion is right, apologize to them for the bad experience they've had and then go to those within your organization to make necessary changes. You must be the biggest cheerleader for your brand. Your people should see your love for them by what you do. No matter how they may act, you are the steward, and you must effectively manage everything that has been placed in your hands with a spirit of excellence.

Those who are managers under you must have that same spirit of excellence as well. It's important that everyone you are leading are speaking the same language. There cannot be two visions. If so, it will breed division. *If you have to keep explaining your vision to certain followers over and over, and they do not help your vision grow, you need to get rid of them. They are a cancer! They will cripple your organization, business or ministry. You must be willing to do this, even if it's a family member.*

Any vision that God gives you, He will place the right people around you who will take your vision as if it's their own and help it to multiply and grow. You must know the condition of your team. Does your team lack performance because of training? If so, you must arm your people with the knowledge they need.

A bad team makes a bad organization. You must pull up any weeds in your garden that is sucking the life out of it. A bad team can develop when the leader does not set clear expectations of what is required. Leaders, you are shooting yourself in the foot if you do not set guidelines.

Leadership requires a lot of maintenance. Once you arrive at your place of work, business, or ministry, your stewardship has just begun. Showing up and being visible is your reasonable service. Making needed changes and alterations to your organization requires the greatest sacrifice but reaps bigger rewards.

Proverbs 27:23-24 says:

23 Be sure you know the condition of your flocks, give careful attention to your herds; 24 for riches do not endure forever, and a crown is not secure for all generations.

You are responsible for the wellbeing of your organization. Be observant of what's going on with your people and your organization. You must know the condition of your flocks, shepherds! Shepherds, you must make an effort to observe what is going on with your flock. Is your flock hurting, discouraged, suicidal, depressed, stressed?

Recognize your people for their positive contributions. Leadership is about selflessness. Put your focus on the Lord and on those who are following you. Your customers, your followers, and your members are stewardship opportunities.

It is also important that your environment has a sweet and organized atmosphere. Set the environment for your people. You cannot stress excellence when your people have terrible working conditions and equipment. Make the needed changes in your environment for your people. This will cause them to love working for you. You cannot continue to function off of 20 to 30-years-old furniture and equipment. Always look to improve and upgrade.

We cannot be afraid of investing in our people. We cannot be afraid of getting hurt or being taking advantage of. If your people are meeting the standards you are setting for them, why not reward them? Why not pay them well? Why not offer them vacation time or sick leave when they need it?

Notice that Proverbs 27:24 says, "for riches do not endure forever, and a crown is not secure for all generations." If you do not stay aware of the condition of your flock, poverty will sneak up on you, and the crown will not be secure for all generations. You cannot leave an inheritance for your family and the generation after you if you do not take care of your flock. Your business, ministry and organization will die if you do not stay abreast of your flock.

I just received a revelation; your checkbook can be your flock as well! Have you balanced your checkbook? Do you know the condition of your financial flock? Are you struggling with debt because you are ignoring the condition of your flock? This is an area that I have battled many times. I loved to shop but did not like to budget. Leaders, we must steward ourselves.

You must make sure that we give a sweet aroma to our people. We must make a concentrated effort to leave what's going on in our personal lives at home. If you have issues too intense and you need some time away to regroup, then please do so. Do not try to be a superhero and not take needed time to refuel. What good is the vision if the visionary is worn out?

You must ask the Lord to help you to be a good steward of your spouse, children, business, ministry, and followers. We cannot ask the Lord to bless us when we have not managed what we have well.

The Greek word for stewardship is *Oikonomis* which means the manager of a household or of household affairs; especially a steward, manager, or superintendent to whom the head of the house or proprietor has entrusted the management of his affairs, the care of receipts and expenditures, and the duty of dealing out the proper portion to every servant and even to children not yet of age. Everything that goes under the roof of a particular house, the house manager is responsible for it.

Leaders, this is why you can't afford to be an invisible leader. You are responsible for everything that is going on under the roof.

Stewardship = Management

Wings #6

Friendships

Friendship is born at that moment when one person says to another, 'What! You too? I thought I was the only one . . .

~ C.S. Lewis

Leadership can be very lonely at times. Because leaders are misunderstood, it can result in that particular leader having to walk alone. I can recall many times during my career where I had to walk alone. Although I loved all of my troops, and I enjoyed talking to them, I still found myself having to walk alone. During my last few assignments, I was truly blessed to meet some amazing friends or what we call in the Air Force, "Wingmen."

Your Wingman is your battle buddy, the one who has your back. Countless times I had to run to my Wingmen for help. They were my sounding board. They were the ones who truly accepted me.

My favorite time of duty day was always lunch. That was the time I could let my hair down and eat out with my friends. For 60 minutes during the duty day, I was Sharon and not Master

Sergeant Johnson. I could not tell you how many times those precious lunch hours with my Wingmen help me keep my sanity.

I have amazing friends outside of the military. My best friend Tajmah has been my "ride or die" friend for over 20 years. She and I met at my first base in North Carolina. I don't know where I would be without her friendship in my life. Tajmah, thank you for teaching me the unconditional love of friendship.

You must take time to invest in your friends. My journey into true friendship started when I was stationed in Los Angeles. I was always a person who was very friendly and cheerful, but I did not have many true friends that I spent a lot of time with. When I arrived at Los Angeles Air Force Base, I met some amazing ladies on my job and at my church, Glory Christian Fellowship International. Pastor Alton and First Lady Trimble I thank you being wonderful shepherds.

During my time at Glory Christian Fellowship, I learned the importance of fellowship. My Pastor loved fellowship. This helped me develop my friendships. I had to learn to allow people to get to know me and to let my walls down. During the duty day, I had three special girlfriends that I loved going to lunch with. We ate together at least one to two times week if our schedules allowed it. It was total therapy for me! My job was very stressful at times and I loved to be able to get way just to vent and de-stress.

During assignment in North Dakota, God blessed me by allowing me to meet even more amazing Wingmen. I miss them right now, and I am so grateful for their friendship!

Leaders, you need time to let your hair down. However, when it comes to personal relationships, everyone cannot handle the real you. It's dangerous to let your hair down in front of the wrong person. You must guard your heart as well as your influence. This will require that we as leaders handle ourselves and our personal lives with discretion.

It takes a special person to handle you with your faults and still respect you as a leader. Only a special breed of people can do this. God has people that He has especially assigned to your life to be your Wingmen.

When God assigns the right people into your life, they will love you with His type of love. They will be able to see past all your flaws and personal issues and help you become a better person. They will not always agree with you and side with you when you are wrong. If you have friends in your life like this, don't let them go.

1 Samuel 1:8 says: "As soon as he had finished speaking to Saul, the soul of Jonathan was knit to the soul of David, and Jonathan loved him as his own soul." This scripture speaks of such a strong bond in friendship that Jonathan loved David like his own soul.

If you have had people who walk away from you, rejoice! Think about it, God said in His word in Hebrews 13:5, "Let your manner of living be without covetousness, and be content with such things as ye have. For He hath said, 'I will never leave thee, nor forsake thee.'"

God promises never to leave us or forsake us, no matter what. He promises to always have our back and to always have our best interest at heart. God is doing us a favor when people are removed from our lives. Favor does not always mean we will get everything. It often means that a lot of things will be kept from us for our good. This is why you must have a strong relationship with God.

We will not always understand why things happen in our lives, but we must understand that God is sovereign. We feel that, although we may appear to lose certain people or things out of our lives, that we must not be favored by God. I beg to differ. Favor also means that certain things will be kept from you, because God knows they are not good for you.

Your prayers must always be for God to remove any and every thing out of your life that is not His best for you. I really believe that if God would peel back the curtains from our lives, we would rejoice and shout. Because He loved us He did not allow us to have everything we wanted. We would be overflowing with gratitude for His protection. It really takes maturity to move on in life when you do not get your way.

God knows the intent of people's hearts. We must trust His will and decision for our lives. We must ask the Lord to give us discernment, so that you will know who is truly for you. My spiritual papa, Prophet Sampson Amoateng, always says, "White teeth does not always mean white heart." You must have discernment. You must be able to recognize the wolves in sheep's clothing.

Healthy friendships should never be a chore to maintain. Friendships should be mutual. There should be a mutual investment within it. If you find that you are investing more into a relationship than the other person, then that relationship is not for you. Relationships are hard work, but it takes two to keep it afloat.

You must be healed in order to become a healthy friend. Your friendships should nourish you and not deplete you. I hate when people say, "I don't need friends; I just need me and Jesus." That is a lie! You do need others, also! People who say this are wounded and using their "relationship" with Christ as a defense mechanism. Never do this, ladies.

We have to be mindful that we, too, have hurt people. We, too, have not always been the perfect friend. If you are in a situation where you had a faithful friend and you have wounded them, then you must apologize and get that right. Leaders, you must take time to cultivate healthy friendships.

Wing #7

Ownership

Ownership: A commitment of the head, heart, and hands to fix the problem and never again affix the blame.

~ John G. Miller

Ownership means the act, state, or right of possessing something. I personally believe that leaders need to operate under a stronger mandate. Leaders, you must take responsibility for whatever is placed in your hands. You must be mature and not pass the buck. We must be sure that everything you do is done in the spirit of excellence.

Leadership is a huge sacrifice. You must have a heart to lead. You must have God's ability to lead. You must have God's super on your natural. Leaders, you must have the spirit of Christ operating in you. He gives you the ability to become a mature leader. There are times you do not feel like leading.

Leaders, you don't just want to be a task finisher but a ground breaker. What good are tasks if you are not breaking new ground? What good is your brand or business if you're not stretching, evolving and changing?

I once heard a powerful man of God, Prophet Russ Walden, say, "You are where your attention takes you." Leaders, if your attention is not first on God, then your family, your business or your ministry, then where is it? You must refocus. There is power in being focused.

Leaders, you must live, breathe and eat excellence and hate mediocrity. I remember one day, around the end of 2016, I was feeling sad about my brand. I felt that it wasn't moving as quickly as I thought it should move. I took responsibility for the fact that I did not do everything that I could have done to help it to grow. I am the type of woman who loves to accomplish things. I have always been a go-getter. The enemy has tried many times to get me to quit. Many days, I went live on Periscope and Facebook live feeling depressed and sad. I was talking to the Lord during one Sunday at church, and I remember asking the Lord to bless my brand.

While riding in the car with my mom to Walmart after church, I shared with her that I heard the Lord tell me earlier during service "Sharon, you are the brand." This was such a light bulb moment for me! I realized that I was separating who I was as a person from my brand. I treated my brand like it was a separate entity from myself. I began to hear the spirit of the Lord say "Sharon, Soar Fly Girl is you. It's your life stories laid bare before the public through books and social media. It's not just your head knowledge, it's you." Soar Fly Girl was the name of my brand from 2016 until October 2017.

The issue of my identity was an area that I battled all my military career. I remembered when people would ask me why I was single, and I would tell them that the Air Force was my husband. I was totally immersed in the military life. I was married to it. It was not the military's fault, it was mine. I totally lost who I was.

I thought, during my career, that the military uniform and the stripes on my arm made me. I felt it was who I was. I had no real confidence in myself without it. This was why my transition out of the military was so difficult. I have cried to God many times and asked Him if I make a mistake by retiring. I asked myself many times, who am I now that I am not military anymore?

Although I am not in anymore, that does not negate who I am. I am created in God's image. I am successful not because of the Air Force but because of what God accomplished in my life through it. The military was not my life, it was just a part of the curriculum God had planned for my life. It was just a wonderful part of my journey but not my final destination.

Many do not understand what veterans go through when they separate and retire. We veterans need your prayers. For many of us, it seems as if we have been stripped and we must totally rebuild our lives and who we are as a person. The military is not evil at all, but it's a very difficult to let go of. Part of it is because of the amazing people and connections.

I began to listen to the voice of God and He explained to me that great potential was in me all the time. He furthered explained that He took me through the path of the military to bring what He has placed in me, out of me. Leaders, here is a big revelation; never despise your small beginnings. Never despise the path that God has you on. It is all part of His plan to develop you. You cannot bring forth a harvest in dry cracked ground. You cannot go into greatness without opposition. God desires that we use the gifts and the talents that He has placed in us to bring Him glory.

Leaders, you are a brand. Whether you are in business or ministry or not. Whether you have or sell products or not. Whether your brand will either grow or die, it is all on you. Your brand is your reputation. Your brand is your behavior. Your brand is how you interact with others. Your brand is what makes you unique and set apart from others.

Leaders, this is why you must have a relationship with God. He is the CEO of your brand. You must have that time with Him to download His plan into you for your life. God knows how to do everything. He knows how to run a business, manage a family, and take care of a ministry. It's not just about making money. It's about the masterpiece that God is creating in you through your surrendered life to Him.

Leaders, you must operate above the norm. Not in pride or in arrogance, but you must know your identity in Him. Honestly speaking, I do not follow a lot of people who do what I do. I do listen to their teaching, but I make sure that I stay true to who God made me to be. I have mentors, but I try to always keep an ear for what God is speaking to me about my brand and my life.

Stay current on things to make your business better. You want to look at what other people in your line of business or ministry are not doing and make that your focus. Do not follow the crowd. Be authentic! That's part of ownership. It's knowing who you are and who you are not and operating in your lane.

Dr. Mike Murdock said during his TV broadcasts that a person who solves a problem is never unemployed. What are the problems that your ministry, business and organization can solve that no else can? As you solve problems in the areas of your business, ministry or organization that no one is doing, you are opening doors towards wealth. This is what will cause people to seek you out and do business with you.

Never copy others or steal their customers or members. Be a leader who constantly evolves. You should be changing and getting better every day. Love who God made you to be. Always look to make needed alterations within your business, ministry and organization.

Deuteronomy 8:17-18 NIV says, *[17] You may say to yourself, 'My power and the strength of my hands have produced this wealth for me.' [18] But remember the Lord your God, for it is he who gives you the ability to produce wealth, and so confirms his covenant, which he swore to your ancestors, as it is today.*

Remember you cannot do it alone. You need God's ability. You need to keep in mind that God is the one who brings you into wealth and not by your own hands. Own your craft! Be mature authentic and responsible leaders!

Wings #8

Helmsmanship

Anyone can steer the ship, but it takes a leader to chart the course. Leaders who are good leaders can take their people almost anywhere.

~ John Maxwell

Welcome to one of my favorite ships. This particular ship was definitely Holy Ghost inspired. I'm sure my Navy vets can identify with this word. Helmsman is defined as a man who steers a ship. A helmsman is also a course plotter. Helmsmanship is the nautical skill or function of a helmsman.

Helm is defined as: 1) Nautical: The steering gear of a ship, especially the tiller or wheel; 2) A position of leadership or control: at the helm of the government, to take the helm of; steer or direct.

A helmsman is an individual who is responsible for the steering of any type of transportation used in or on the water. A professional helmsman may serve on a submarine, a private vessel such as a yacht or sailboat, or a military vessel such as a ship or aircraft carrier. It is the responsibility of helmsmen to carry out the orders of the captain in terms of plotting courses and making sure the vessel arrives and departs at various ports in a timely manner.

James 3:1-5 International Standard Version says, *[1]Not many of you should become teachers, my brothers, because you know that we who teach will be judged more severely than others. ²For all of us make many mistakes. If someone does not make any mistakes when he speaks, he is perfect and able to control his whole body. ³Now if we put bits into horses' mouths to make them obey us, we can guide their whole bodies as well. ⁴And look at ships! They are so big that it takes strong winds to drive them, yet they are steered by a tiny rudder wherever the* **helmsman** *directs. ⁵In the same way, the tongue is a small part of the body, yet it can boast of great achievements. A huge forest can be set on fire by a little flame. Although ships are large in size and appear unmanageable, it's because of a small rudder a large ship can be directed to turn whichever way the helmsman directs it. He who controls the rudder controls the ship!*

This scripture talks about the power of the tongue. This scripture is so powerful. It's important that you control your tongue. A leader who controls his tongue controls his ship!

Leaders, your words have power. Leaders, direction comes out of your mouth; instruction comes out of your month. You must be a wise helmsman. You must be able to get your character and words under control.

Leaders, your personal life is just as important as your public/professional life. Your character is revealed by the words you speak. You are labeled by your words and your actions. Remember, you are a brand. When your character and speech is not in order, you are killing your brand! Do you not know that when you speak curse words, you are actually opening yourself up for a curse? Why is it that when you curse, it's low level words? Saying these kinds words release curses and destruction over your life. This is an area that you must ask God to cleanse you from. Use your words to build up and not tear down. Your words have power leaders. What have you been saying lately? What have you been saying about your career, business or ministry?

Ladies, cursing is not attractive! I am speaking from experience. Gentlemen calling a woman the "b" word is not becoming. Ladies, referring to yourself as the "b" word is not cute. You are degrading yourself and other ladies. By cursing, you are releasing a curse over a life. You are opening yourself up in the spirit realm for poverty, lack, and other curses to come upon you when you constantly curse. You are speaking the Devil's language when you are cursing. Leaders, your words carry power. Your words should be used to build up and not to curse. Your tongue is a small member, but wrong words bring your brand down in a blaze. It may not be a physical blaze but it is unraveling in the realm of the Spirit.

Leaders, you must always posture yourself for God to move in your life. If your heart is not pure, you will destroy your ship which is your brand. Leaders, you must be able to carry yourself professionally. You must learn how to carry yourself so that greatness can be released in your life. Your words depict your character.

Kings issue decrees by words. So leaders, begin to use your words to guide your people, give direction, and build your brand. Use your words to worship God. Speak life and not death over your career, family, business, ministry, and relationships. Use your words to bless and not curse.

Do not be a rude and critical leader. Do not be a verbally abusive leader. Steer your ship! Look at it this way, your ship is your brand and all of those who have been placed in your hands to influence. Those who work for you need to be the same type of people. You should not tolerate any destructive conversations when it comes to your brand.

Another point that I would like to make is that a good helmsman takes control of the ship and keeps the ship on course. You must stay on course and not be distracted. You must listen for the voice of the Lord and follow His direction. A wise helmsman is able to stay steady when there are rough winds. A good helmsman has charted out his destination and stays on course. With the help of the Lord, as you stay on course, He will help you to get to where you need to go. God is aware of everything that you will face in your life. But you must receive instruction from Him so that you can avoid the rocks that are ahead in life. You must have Christ as the Helmsman of your life. He must drive you in every area of your life. Without Him, your ship will be destroyed.

So leaders. who is in control of your ship? Is Jesus in control of your ship or yourself? With Jesus at the helm of your boat, you will reach your destination on schedule!

Some things are waves and not storms. Ride the wave and do not lose focus. I love the song Jesus Take the Wheel by Carrie Underwood. Jesus must take the wheel in your life. As you allow Him to control your ship inward, it will help you outwardly. He gives you the ability to survive the roughest waves. As you feed your inner man in prayer, reading and worship, you will grow. You will become a better and more effective leader.

So fellow helmsmen, you must do some inventory and decide who you will allow to drive your boat. Surrender to Him. Allow him to chart your course. God wants to place your brand on display for the world to see!

Wing #9

Shipwrecks

A ship is safe in a harbor, but that is not what a ship is built for.

~ Grace Murray Hopper

Leaders, we must be prepared to encounter the unexpected. We must be prepared to face challenges or unexpected tragedies. We all are familiar with the tragic story of the Titanic. Although this event was very tragic, the Titanic is more famous because of tragedy. During my research, I found out an eye-opening discovery. There was a ship called the SS Californian, which sent out warning messages to the Titanic regarding packed ice ahead. The SS Californian was only a few miles from the Titanic. A wireless operator by the name of James Phillips ignored the warnings. This failure caused Captain Edward Smith not to receive the proper information in order to take proper action to save all of his crew and passengers.

There is another side to this story. "Testimony before the British inquiry revealed that at 10:10 p.m., the Californian observed the lights of a ship to the south; it was later agreed between Captain Stanley Lord and Third Officer C.V. Groves (who had relieved Lord of duty at 11:10 p.m.) that this was a passenger liner. At 11:50 p.m., the officer had watched that ship's lights flash out, as if she had shut down or turned sharply, and that the port light was now visible.

Morse light signals to the ship, upon Lord's order, were made between 11:30 p.m. and 1:00 a.m., but were acknowledged. If the Titanic were as far from the Californian as Lord claimed, then he knew, or should have known, that Morse signals would not be visible. A reasonable and prudent course of action would have been to awaken the wireless operator and to instruct him to attempt to contact Titanic by that method. Had Lord done so, it is possible that he could have reached Titanic in time to save additional lives.

Leaders, it is critical that you are prepared in the case of shipwrecks. The Titanic's shipwreck could have been totally preventable. During times of leading, you will have many icebergs and other events which will come against you to destroy your boat. It is pertinent that your faith in God remains intact. A wrong decision, connection or relationship can wreck your whole ship.

On the other hand, you could have done all that you could have done to walk upright and with integrity, and you would still experience a shipwreck. Shipwrecks could be betrayal by a friend or a relative, divorce, separation, bankruptcy, or a death of someone who is close you. These are things that come into your life out of nowhere and totally blind side you. This can happen whether it is your fault or not.

Apostle Paul in Acts 27: 21-25 shows the perfect example of how to handle the many shipwrecks of leadership. Below is an excerpt from the sermon, Leadership Lessons From Paul's Shipwreck, which outlined six leadership characteristics that Paul displayed.

1. Expected the unexpected.

    A. Paul expected what others never expected (Acts 27:9-12).

    B. He was a visionary leader. He wasn't driven by what he saw (Acts 27:13).

C. Ask God for wisdom that you will see crisis in advance and prepare yourself.

2. Remembered God's purpose.

A. Paul was aware of God's plan and purpose (Acts 9:15-16).

B. He shrewdly appealed to Caesar and arranged to sail to Rome so that he could preach to Romans! (Acts 27:23-25).

C. When in crisis, remember God's purpose. It helps to maintain focus on the mission.

3. Took control of the situation.

A. Paul didn't blame but had faith in God and sustained hope (Acts 27:21-25).

B. He assumed leadership, took control and devised a plan (Acts 27:26).

C. Leaders are called to sustain hope, control situations, devise plans and take action.

4. Maintained a composed attitude.

A. In the middle of havoc, Paul gathers a pile of brushwood. A sign of composed attitude (Acts 28:3).

B. It is Paul's composed attitude that gave him the ability to lead his team.

C. Leaders with composed attitudes always win the trust of their followers.

5. Remembered his identity.

A. The Maltese were swift to judge. They believed Paul was a criminal and later a god, (Acts 28:3-6).

B. Paul wasn't concerned. He knew he was neither a sinner, nor a god. Rather used the opportunity to minister.

    C. When criticized, leaders must remember their identity in God because seeking to silence the critics distracts you from the task.

6. Didn't stop leading.

    A. The bad weather forced Paul to stay in Malta for three months.

    B. He continued to lead instead of sitting idle and cursing the weather (Acts 28:8-11).

    C. Real leaders transform crisis into new opportunities for leading.

Be sure to take an opportunity and seriously study the scriptures from the outline above. No matter what you are facing, God knows how to cause you to avoid disaster. Shipwrecks in our lives can also become blessings. Many of us may have experienced some shipwrecks that have saved our lives. Many of us may have needed shipwrecks because we did not heed the warnings that He has given us. I cannot tell you how many times I was forewarned and did not heed the messages that God was showing me. I ran into many icebergs in my life. Many of them were unnecessary.

Leaders, you need to have sharp eagle eye vision. It is important that you ask the Lord for discernment. Lack of discernment will cost you time, money and relationships. Remember, you are building a brand, you cannot afford to shipwreck unnecessarily. You must spend quality time with the Lord. He is the one who sees what icebergs are ahead of you. Just because an iceberg appears small above water, does not mean it should be ignored. Icebergs are normally massive underneath the water. If you are shipwrecked, do not weep and cry over your old ship, allow the Lord to help you to rebuild a new one!

Wing #10

Fellowship

Leaders must bond with other leaders. Leaders must bounce leadership ideas and issues around with other leaders.

~ Tom Deighan

Leaders, you must embrace fellowship. A major facet of fellowship is spending time with like-minded people. Leaders, you must be fellowship with other leaders. Fellowship includes getting to know your fellow peers. The Greek word for fellowship is Koinonia.

Many think that fellowship is just sitting around the table in front of a well-prepared meal. But true fellowship is beyond a meal. It is connecting like-minded people. As believers, we fellowship together, because we have one common bond, which is Jesus Christ.

Leaders, you need to fellowship with other leaders. This past weekend I had the pleasure of attending a Ministers' Clinic for the Church of God Presbytery. During this clinic, I met some great brothers and sisters who have had an array of experiences in ministry. What I really liked about this clinic was that the focus was not on the people that we were leading; it was on us as ministers and how we needed to become better. I found it comforting to listen to the stories of ministers and pastors who have served in the ministry for much longer than I have. I learned a lot from listening to those who have served in the trenches of ministry. Although I have never pastored, I was still able to glean and learn from those who did.

I felt such a connection to them because of the common bond we shared together. We not only learned together, but we also broke bread together. When great leaders fellowship with other great leaders, there is a sharpening that happens. Getting to know other great leaders will help you to form better bonds and stronger connections.

Leaders, you must be able to get to know other leaders. Many times, it is so easy to pour out and meet the needs of others that we fail to meet our own needs. One of the biggest needs we have is connection. We were created by God to connect. Connecting with other leaders can also increase networking connections. The more people you connect with, the greater your connections. This was what I valued most during my time in the Air Force.

Connections can help make your leadership connections much better. As I sat in the Minister's Clinic, I also valued how the ministers began to share and encourage one another. This was because we understood what each other was going through. That's why you need fellowship leaders. You need camaraderie. You need to have connection.

Fellowshipping in the right circles can cause you to receive some golden nuggets of information to aid in you in your business or brand. Fellowshipping can also bring much needed peace of mind. Leadership can be lonely and there is comfort to any leader to be understood and supported. Again precious leaders, you must be able to connect. When you think of fellowship, it's beyond just your family. Again, it's with those whom you share a common bond.

Wing #11

Kinship

Kinship – not serving the other but being one with the other. Jesus was not "a man for others;" he was one with them. There is a world of difference in that.

~ Gregory Boyle

Kinship means the state or fact of being of kin, such as a family relationship. It also means relationship by nature and qualities. During my time in the Air Force, I was often asked, "Who is your next of kin?" I was asked this because they needed to know the nearest family member to contact in case of emergency.

Leaders, your relationship with your family is your most important relationship. God has given you an opportunity to lead in order to lead your family into the next level. Many leaders place success ahead of their families. They place their confidence in success and worship money more than maintaining connections with their families.

Listen, leaders, whether you have a good family or a bad family you need to maintain your relationships with your family. You can lead more effectively when you get all of your skeletons out of your closet. Many of your skeletons come from bad relationships with family members. Many of us are leading and broken, leading and wounded, and finally leading and angry. This happened to me the majority of my career. I spent most of it wounded, rejected and angry. This was because of childhood issues that I did not deal with. My troops felt the brunt of it many times. Broken leaders produce broken followers.

Although I had a very successful career, made a lot of money, and had many awards, I was still not whole as a woman. See leaders, you are a woman first. You must be whole. You must be healed and delivered from the past. The root of my wounds was a broken relationship. I stuffed it down and tried to perform in spite of it but, like a sore thumb, it was still there.

Leaders, when things aren't right at home, things will not flow right with your brand. Your influence depends on your relationships, not only with those you lead, but also with your family. Your family knows the real you. Your family knows who you are in spite of your title and your success. For some of you having a good relationship with your family is very difficult. I totally understand. At the same time, you must deal with it so that you can lead as a "whole" woman.

The fact that you are still hanging on to what is happening to you is stunting the growth of your brand. Remember leaders, you are a brand. You must ask yourself if you treat those you lead in your business or ministry better than you treat your own family? Do you love on your flock more than your family, shepherds? Are you one way in front of others and an abusive monster at home? Your family life is your most primary relationship. Your family is how you learn to interact with others.

Some of us come from an abusive family so, therefore, we physically or verbally abuse others. Sit down right now and really ask yourself if you have two faces. Do you have multiple personalities? Do you put on such a façade that your family does not know who you are in public? Do you spend more time with your business or ministry than your own family? Has your ministry or business replaced or became your spouse?

My request to you today is to stop sweeping this issue under the rug. Stop trying to succeed broken. The spotlight will only shine light on who you really are. Fame will only put you and your family more into the limelight. This is why you must get things right behind closed doors. We must fix those broken relationships before we get to the top. If you do not deal with those areas now, you are opening the door to scandal.

This is also a part of being a person of integrity. You must incorporate integrity within your brand. The Holy Spirit just spoke to me, too, that it would be wise to interview those who are working for you as well. Family issues are the biggest distractions to any successful employee. If things at home are not right, then things at your business or ministry will not be right. I am not, by any means, advocating to fire people who have issues, but it's always best to seek out ways to assist others. Most of the time, they will need outside counseling. If it is in your ability to help them get the help they need, then offer it.

First, make sure you are getting the help that you need. As I speak about this, you must ask yourself, what do I need to do to move on? Do you need to confront someone? Do you need to pick of the phone and call? Do you need to visit your estranged family members? Do you need to ask for forgiveness from your family? I am sure you are saying, "Sharon, you don't know how my family is." No, I don't know them, but this will only help you move forward in the end. You must deal with this issue and have that dreaded conversation with your loved ones.

When you do deal with it, you must come with the mindset that if they accept you, fine; if not, still fine. Allow the one who hurt you to explain why they did it or why they did nothing about it to help you. If you don't feel comfortable talking to that person one on one, then seek help from a therapist to assist you, but you must confront. Trust and believe that you will be a better leader and individual because of it.

On the other hand, seek to build stronger ties with your family. Seek out opportunities to draw closer to them. Make it a point to have dinner dates with your spouse. Make time to sit at the table and eat dinner together daily or weekly. Call and visit your siblings and your parents to check on them. Your parents are very important, do not neglect them. Do not throw them away no matter how badly you were treated. You may have to distance yourself depending on the situation but don't throw them away. Find time to ask your children what is going on with them in school. Make it your goal to become more engaged. Don't just do it this week. Make this a lifetime change. Make sure you take care of home first!

Your family will thank you for it later. 1 Timothy 3:5 says, "For if a man does not know how to manage his own family, how can he take care of God's church?" This scripture really sums it up. How can you take care of the things of God and not take care of your family?

Leaders, you are the trendsetter for the next generation. With God's help, you can become a bondage breaker. You can show your family that with God you can be prosperous spiritually and financially. What legacy are you planting for your children? Are you teaching them about business? Are you teaching them to have good relationships? Are you teaching them about the Lord? What legacy are you leaving to the rest of your family? What can they say that you left behind with the family's name on it after you are long gone?

Are you a redeemer or a destroyer? Are you using your influence to impact and help your family? Today, let this be your "aha" moment. Build your family and strengthen your brand. Strengthen your leadership abilities by getting things right at home. This will help you to lead more effectively with peace and greater wisdom.

Wing #12

Worship

*If you make history with God while no one is watching, God will make history with
you while everyone is watching.*

~ Bill Johnson

Worship is the act of giving reverent honor and homage to God. Leaders, worship must a part of your everyday life. Worship strengthens your relationship and connection with God. Leaders must have a hearing and understanding heart. Worship opens your heart to receive instruction for your life, your brand, and your relationships. We must not just box worship for Sundays only. God is still God Mondays through Saturdays.

If you are just worshipping God on Sundays only, you are limiting yourself to just being religious. Your relationship with God should be top priority in your life. If you do not have a relationship with God or don't know how to worship, we will talk about that later in this chapter.

Leaders, when I speak of hearing God, I am not saying that you should just sit there. Hearing God is about getting in His presence and allowing Him to speak and to download into you. Do you not know that God has ideas and thoughts that He wants to share with you? Do you not know that God has ideas that can take your life, career, brand or ministry to the next level?

Remember that you are your brand. Your brand cannot grow past you and the team that you have around you. As a leader, you must have discernment. You must be able to see past things and people who appear to be good to what is behind it. Many leaders have lost opportunities, money and time because of lack of discernment. Please understand that I am not advocating looking at every opportunity and person that comes into your life with the side eye. What I am saying is that when those persons or opportunities present themselves to you, take them to your head "CEO" - God.

Let's discuss 1 Kings 7:3-15:

3 Solomon showed his love for the Lord by walking according to the instructions given him by his father David, except that he offered sacrifices and burned incense on the high places. 4 The king went to Gibeon to offer sacrifices, for that was the most important high place, and Solomon offered a thousand burnt offerings on that altar. 5 At Gibeon the Lord appeared to Solomon during the night in a dream, and God said, "Ask for whatever you want me to give you." 6 Solomon answered, "You have shown great kindness to your servant, my father David, because he was faithful to you and righteous and upright in heart. You have continued this great kindness to him and have given him a son to sit on his throne this very day.

7 "Now, Lord my God, you have made your servant king in place of my father David. But I am only a little child and do not know how to carry out my duties. 8 Your servant is here among the people you have chosen, a great people, too numerous to count or number. 9 So give your servant a discerning heart to govern your people and to distinguish between right and wrong. For who is able to govern this great people of yours?" 10 The Lord was pleased that Solomon had asked for this. 11 So God said to him, "Since you have asked for this and not for long life or wealth for yourself, nor have asked for the death of your enemies but for discernment in administering justice, 12 I will do what you have asked. I will give you a wise and discerning heart,

so that there will never have been anyone like you, nor will there ever be. 13 Moreover, I will give you what you have not asked for—both wealth and honor—so that in your lifetime you will have no equal among kings. 14 And if you walk in obedience to me and keep my decrees and commands as David your father did, I will give you a long life." 15 Then Solomon awoke—and he realized it had been a dream.

Solomon was the son of one of the most prominent worshippers in the Bible. David had 13 sons; Solomon was his tenth son. Upon David's death, Solomon became king of Israel. David was known to be a worshipper. I really believed that Solomon saw the lifestyle of his father and he did what he was taught. David died at the age of 70 and passes on the throne to Solomon at the age of 12 who reigned for 40 years.

This young man exercised great reverence for God. This man also had the greatest task of building a temple for God. He finished the vision that his father could not do. Solomon worshipped God by giving Him huge sacrifices in the high places. In other words, he worshipped God so strong that He got God's attention until God told him to ask for whatever he wanted.

Can you imagine living such a life worship that it provokes God to say, "What must I do for you"? There is nothing greater than getting God's attention. Solomon pulled on God's heart strings. Worship is God's heart strings.

Leaders, you must seek for God's attention more than man's attention. This is why you must worship. Most importantly, you must worship with a pure heart with no ulterior motives other than genuine love for God. God's offer to Solomon was a heavy request. Can you imagine God asking that question to you? If so, what would you ask? Solomon understood that he was a young man and that ruling Israel was a heavy responsibility. He did not attend king college, he did not attend king high school. He did not have a Bachelor's or Master's degree in kingship. He knew that he had limitations. A wise leader always understands their limitations; therefore, they seek to surround themselves with those who excel in the areas where they are weak.

Leaders, the most important person you must have in your corner is God! Solomon asked God to give him a wise and understanding heart. God responds to Solomon that because he did not ask for riches, God hooked him up! According to verses 12 and 13 He gave what he asked for and what he did not ask for. God not only gave Solomon wisdom, but He also gave him wealth.

Ladies, this is your key to a million dollar brand! You need wisdom to run your company or ministry. You need God to tell you who to connect with and who not to connect with. He put your brand, company, or ministry in you in the first place for His glory.

Wisdom requires hearing and obeying the voice of God! Leaders, be sure to meditate on this chapter. Study Solomon's heart and his character. Solomon asked God for characteristics that he needed from God that he did not have.

Things later changed for Solomon. Not because of God, but because he turned away from worshipping God. God forewarned Solomon in 1 Kings 9: 4-9 not to turn away and worship other Gods.

1 Kings 9: 4-9 says:

4 As for you, if you walk before me faithfully with integrity of heart and uprightness, as David your father did, and do all I command and observe my decrees and laws, 5 I will establish your royal throne over Israel forever, as I promised David your father when I said, 'You shall never fail to have a successor on the throne of Israel.' 6 'But if you or your descendants turn away from me and do not observe the commands and decrees I have given you and go off to serve other gods and worship them, 7 then I will cut off Israel from the land I have given them and will reject this temple I have consecrated for my Name. Israel will then become a byword and an object of ridicule among all peoples. 8 This temple will become a heap of rubble. All who pass by will be appalled and will scoff and say, 'Why has the Lord done such a thing to this land and to this temple?' 9 People will answer, 'Because they have forsaken the Lord their God, who brought their ancestors out of Egypt, and have embraced other gods, worshiping and serving them—that is why the Lord brought all this disaster on them.

God gives Solomon fair warning not to embrace other gods. God was not operating in arrogance. He wanted Solomon not to disconnect from the source of his wisdom. Solomon later married women who did not serve God. This is where you begin to see Solomon unravel. His worship began to shift from God to other gods. He allowed his love of women who did not serve God to cause him to worship other gods. Solomon continued to unravel and later died.

Leaders, you must not allow anyone or anything to pull you away from God. Therefore, you must worship God every day. You must set aside time to spend in the presence of God.

Special Thank You:

I would like to personally thank everyone of you for purchasing my book. I personally believe that God handpicked all of you to buy this book. I pray that you received a life changing deposit and that you will never "lead" the same again. Please accept my invitation to join my **12 Wings of Successful Business Leadership Closed Group** on Facebook. I would love to hear about your thoughts regarding this book and to get to know you more. In this group we will go further and dig out even more nuggets from my book. See you in the group!

Special Prayer For You:

Prayer for Military Leaders:

Father In The Name of Jesus, I lift every military leader before you. I pray that You will protect her as she serves to protect this great nation. I pray that she will be a positive example and groom every troop to reach their highest potential. I pray that she will always make wise decisions and wear her uniform proudly. I pray that she will see the greatness that You have placed on the inside of her and that she will abide by the rules of those placed over her. I pray that she will not allow stressful work environments she may work in to cause her to become hard to those she lead. I pray that she will learn to cultivate positive relationships so that she can flourish and soar in everything that she does. May she exemplify professionalism and always listen to Your voice when she is face with obstacles. We thank you Lord and we call it done in Jesus name amen.

Prayer for Marketplace Professional Women:

Father In The Name of Jesus, Lord I thank you for this mighty professional/business woman. I pray that as she goes about her day that she will be focused, productive and soar in excellence. I pray that she balances her professional and personal life. I pray that you will bless her to manage what you have placed in her hands with wisdom and discretion. I pray that You give her insight and mighty ideas to do that things that no one in her profession has ever done. May she not seek to compete with others within her market. Keep her eyes fix on what You are doing in her life and career. May she wax great in wisdom and wealth. I pray that as you groom her in Your presence that men and women will be drawn to her and seek her out because of the spirit of excellence that is on her life. May pride and arrogance be far from her. May she always keep her hands clean and handle business honestly in Jesus name amen.

Prayer for Women In Ministry:

Father In the Name of Jesus, Lord I thank you for the Woman of God reading this prayer right now. Bless her Lord as she pours out to others. Ministry is very demanding and many times thankless. I pray that she will remember that you are the one who rewards us. Lord, I pray that this vessel will continue to stand for what is right and that she will grow in Godly relationships. May she preach and minister under the guidance and the authority of your Holy Spirit May she not become weary in well doing. May she be a faithful woman who always abound in blessings. According to Jeremiah 18:8 may she be like a tree planted by the water that sends out its roots by the stream. It does not fear when heat comes; its leaves are always green. May she preach and minister boldly under your anointing. Help her to remember to stay filled with your with your Spirit so that she will always have a reservoir for those who need her and for herself. In Jesus Name Amen.

Air Force Veteran * Leadership Coach * Minister * Motivational Speaker

Website: www.elevatehiher.org

Email: sharon@elevatehiher.org

<u>Available Services:</u>

One on One Leadership Coaching

Leadership Group Coaching

Motivational Speaking

Conferences/Seminars/Workshops

Church Conferences/Training/Events

Webinars

Let's Stay Connected!

I would like to personally invite you to follow me on any of my social media channels:

Periscope: SharonRJHarris

Facebook: Elevate Hi-HER

Instagram: Elevate Hiher

Sources

Introduction

http://www.dictionary.com/browse/-ship

http://www.webster-dictionary.net/definition/leadership

https://www.ideaconnection.com/blog/2014/04/open-innovation-commitment/

Chapter 1

http://www.kingjamesbibleonline.org/Hebrews-Chapter-11/

http://www.wisdomquotes.com/quote/james-kouzes-and-barry-posner-4.html

http://www.biblestudytools.com/nlt/proverbs/passage/?q=proverbs+27:23-24

Chapter 2

http://www.biblestudytools.com/nlt/proverbs/29-14.html

https://www.biblegateway.com/passage/?search=Proverbs+22%3A6&version=NIV

Chapter 3

http://www.dictionary.com/browse/craftsmanship

https://www.thindifference.com/2013/11/leadership-craft/

Chapter 4

http://www.leadershipnow.com/followershipquotes.html

https://www.merriam-webster.com/dictionary/followership

http://www.relationshipskills.com/resources/Biblical-Followership.pdf

https://www.biblegateway.com/passage/?search=1+Kings+19%3A19 -21&version=NIV

Chapter 5

http://biblehub.com/greek/3623.htm

https://www.biblegateway.com/passage/?search=Proverbs+27%3A23 -27&version=NIV

Chapter 6

http://www.searchquotes.com/quotation/Friendship_is_born_at_that _moment_when_one_person_says_to_another%2C_%27What%21_Y ou_too%3F_I_thought_I_was_t/511/#ixzz4X3wyCK13

http://danblackonleadership.info/archives/2143

https://www.biblegateway.com/passage/?search=1+Samuel+18&versi on=ESV

https://www.biblegateway.com/verse/en/Hebrews%2013%3A5

Chapter 7

http://www.bing.com/search?FORM=SK216DF&PC=SK216&q=ow nership+definition

https://www.biblegateway.com/passage/?search=Deuteronomy+8%3 A17-18&version=NIV

Chapter 8

http://www.thefreedictionary.com/helmsmanship

http://www.thefreedictionary.com/helm

https://www.scribd.com/document/88552046/The-Helmsman-2

Chapter 9

https://en.wikipedia.org/wiki/RMS_Titanic#Wreck

http://www.virtualpreacher.org/sermon-outlines/leadership-lessons-pauls-shipwreck/

Chapter 10

https://sites.google.com/site/schoolleaderbiblestudy2/slbs-devotionals/fellowshipofleadersleaningoneachother

Chapter 11

https://www.goodreads.com/quotes/tag/kinship

http://www.dictionary.com/browse/kinship

Chapter 12

https://www.pinterest.com/explore/worship-quotes/

https://www.biblegateway.com/passage/?search=1+Kings+3%3A7-12&version=NIV

https://www.gotquestions.org/sons-of-David.html

https://www.biblegateway.com/passage/?search=1%20Kings+11&version=NIV

https://www.biblegateway.com/passage/?search=romans10%3A8-9&version=NKJV